The Answers:
A Parent's Guide to Discussing Racism with Children

Troya Bishop, M.Ed.

Copyright © 2018 Bishop Global Education & Consulting, LLC

All rights reserved.

ISBN: 978-0-9821468-0-4

DEDICATION

This book is dedicated to all of the children in this world. Especially to my daughter Zoe: you are my love, my inspiration and my joy. I pray that this book will encourage conversations that bring healing, so the world is a better place for you and many generations of my legacy that follow you. God is with you to protect you, He is sovereign, and He is just. Always remember that.

This book is also dedicated to my godchildren: Malcolm, Micah, Jace, & Jorian. I love you, and I pray that God will shelter you as you navigate through this world. I have faith in the wisdom that your parents and I have shared with you. I also have faith that our God will guide and keep you.

To all of my little cousins, and my nieces and nephews: I love ya'll too, and I know all of you will reap the benefits of the adults who read this book, teach their children, and begin to tear down racism. God Bless You!

CONTENTS

	Dedication	i
	Acknowledgments	ii
0	Preface: How to Use This Book	p. 3
1	Framing the Discussion	p. 7
2	Use Appropriate Vocabulary	p. 11
3	Be a Positive Role Model	p. 17
4	Embrace Diversity	p. 24
5	Develop a Strong Sense of Self-Identity	p. 30
6	Embrace Family History	p. 35
7	Encourage Curiosity	p. 39
8	Implications	p. 43
9	Conclusion	p. 48
10	A Conversation with Black Men	p. 56
11	Reference Section	p. 92
12	About the Author	p.100

ACKNOWLEDGMENTS

I must begin by acknowledging a few people who have helped to shape me, and who have encouraged me to live in the freedom of "authenticity". I do my best to be who I believe God purposed me to be, and to speak the truth as I see it.

My first acknowledgement is my love for a man whose life I have studied and have found to be fascinating: my Lord and Savior, Jesus Christ. To my parents, my sister, and my friends & family (too many to name), you know I love you and appreciate your support.

To my supporters and friends at Central High School, Howard University, Tennessee State University, Hustle University, Novae Life, and Hip Hop Speakz Radio Show, thank you! Your encouraging words and kind deeds mean more to me than words can express. Very special thank you to the editing team: Mrs. Eugene Edwards and Mr. Barry Brown.

Finally I would like to thank the scholars whose works I have studied and used to help me in the process of healing from the ills of racism: Dr. Na'im Akbar, Dr. Frances Cress Welsing, Dr. Claud Anderson, Dr. Phillp McGraw, Dr. John Henrik Clarke, Dr. Maya Angelou, Dr. Cornell West, Bishop TD Jakes, Evangelist Joyce Meyer, Self Esteem Development Coach Haziq Ali, and Professor Tim Wise.

PREFACE
HOW TO USE THIS BOOK
GIVE YOURSELF PERMISSION TO THINK FREELY

It may seem a bit ambiguous for me to tell adults how to use a book. Naturally, I understand the humor in that statement. However, I want to make sure that you as parents are equipped to have "the race talk" with your kids and perhaps friends and family members, in the most appropriate, effective ways. The most effective way to teach adults how to do anything, is by using critical thinking (Brookfield, 2004).

Critical thinking focuses primarily on two types of assumptions: power assumptions and hegemonic assumptions. **Power assumptions** influence how we view power and relationships in our lives. **Hegemonic assumptions** influence how we embrace particular thoughts, because we believe those thoughts are in our own best interest. Hegemonic assumptions actually work against us in the long term, because they serve the interests of those who do not have our best interest at heart (Brookfield, 2004). As a process for reading this book, I challenge you as parents to determine what your assumptions are, and to challenge those assumptions. I invite you to ask as many questions as possible as you read, and write them down.

This book has a companion workbook, with a corresponding chapter for each chapter in the book. If you have a partner or friend to work on the exercises with you, please engage them through the process. Talk freely, share honestly, and write your answers down. You may be surprised to see how your perspective changes each time you refer to the guide for suggestions. Read the book slowly, taking time to reflect and write after each chapter.

It took me more than 30 years to develop my thoughts and learn from my experiences. It has also taken me a few months to synthesize the research that's included in this book. It is my intention, to give you facts from other scholars and experts, and not solely my emotions or opinions. I will emphasize the critical thinking aspect of this guide. After each chapter, put the book aside. Take some time to reflect on your experiences and what you've read. Record your thoughts in your workbook. Essentially, take time to do some research on your own.

In the age of information and technology, there are plenty of avenues to assist you in finding a deeper understanding of racism in the culture of the United States. The books and articles included in the reference section (of this book) are a great starting point. If you don't have access to ERIC (U.S. Dept. of Education) or other educational databases where peer-reviewed articles are found, most public libraries have access to those resources at no cost to library patrons.

Once you complete the guide and workbook, you will have a more clear idea with where to begin the conversation about race with your children. You will also have the appropriate vocabulary to do so. The accompanying coloring book and situational gaming cards will help guide you in this discussion with your children. They also provide a tool to give your children what they want the most, which is quality time with their parents.

After completing the above suggestions, you will be equipped with the tools you need to talk to your children about racism. You will be confident, and you will do your part in ending racism in your own way. We _will_ make this country better, together!

Troya Bishop, M. Ed.

CHAPTER 1
FRAMING THE DISCUSSION
HOW DO HUMANS RESPOND TO OPPRESSION?

Prior to examining the topic of racism and guiding our children through that discussion, we as adults must first examine primary components of racism that are universal. This examination will help frame our discussion. Two underlying components of racism are poverty and oppression. Oppressed and impoverished people have responded to oppression and poverty in ways that are consistent, regardless of ethnic group and geographical location. The psychological nature of human response to social constructs (i.e. oppression, poverty, etc.) has been consistent for thousands of years. If we examine oppressed and impoverished people in Africa, Asia, Australia, or Europe, from the beginning of recorded history until present day; we will find consistent ways that people who were oppressed (or in poverty) responded to their social condition. With that historical framework in mind, it is essential to define oppression and poverty.

According to Merriam-Webster's Dictionary, oppression is the unjust or cruel use of authority or power (2015). They define poverty as, the state of one who lacks a standard or socially acceptable amount of money or material possessions. With those definitions in mind, let's ask ourselves a few questions:

- Have Black/African American people historically been oppressed in America?
- Have Black/African American people historically been impoverished in America?
- Have Black/African American people responded to oppression in ways similar to other oppressed people in the world?
- Have Black/African American people responded to poverty in ways similar to other impoverished people in the world?

If you are unsure about the answer to any of these questions or answered, "no," to any of these questions, it may be a good idea to research European, African, Australian, or Asian history (beginning with the first or second century). A review of American history prior to the Civil War may be helpful as well. Again, the idea is to approach the topic of racism from a historical, humanistic perspective. In doing so, we will help relieve biases and preconceptions about other ethnic groups. It will also help us derive realistic and practical ways to relate the complexities of racism in simple terms, to our children.

I raise all of the prior points, because the topic of racism in America is often approached in the framework of, "What's wrong with Black people," or "What Black people should be doing is…". I wholeheartedly reject that approach, which dehumanizes African Americans. I believe the delicate subject should be approached from the lens of humanity and with humility; not superiority or arrogance. When making comparisons to assess progress or to determine future outcomes, most people easily agree that a fair comparison should be made. Whether comparing fruit, apples to apples, or a student's test scores, a first grader to a first grader, we must make sure that we are comparing things or subjects that are alike. In this work, I insist that we compare African Americans only to other ethnic groups who have historically been subjected to poverty and oppression.

My approach to this massive subject is with great humility and a deep commitment to learning more about myself, my biases and my history. I pledge to use the knowledge I gain to make my future and the future of my children and grandchildren, better and more just.

I encourage each person reading this book to share my commitment to learning more about yourself, your biases, and your history. This is a guide for us as parents, to help our children relate to people who are different from them and their family members. It is my hope that each parent will also approach this conversation with humility, and an intentional commitment to being authentic and becoming a better human being. I hope that same sentiment is passed on to our children as we engage them in conversation and teach them to do their part in ending racism and bringing more peace to the earth.

CHAPTER 2
USE APPROPRIATE VOCABULARY
DEFINITIONS FOR OUR DISCUSSION. WHAT IS RACISM?

Racism is both an idea and a system (Wise, 2015). It is the belief that certain people have characteristics or abilities, which make them superior to other groups of people. Racism is wielding power over another person or group of people (West, 2015). Therefore, people without power, cannot be racist. As a system, racism is an arranged institution that is maintained by practices, procedures, and policies (Wise, 2015). Racism is also treating people unfairly. Fairness is In this book, as a system it is referred to as institutional racism.

Institutional racism is both formal and informal, and results in some people having more opportunity than others and better treatment than others, directly based on their ethnic background (i.e. the color of their skin). Institutional racism also involves denying people opportunities, rewards, or benefits on the basis of ethnic background or "race," to which those individuals are otherwise entitled. Plainly, racism is a system of bullying, based on how people look. I also want to define the word *race*, as it will be referred to often in this book.

In the United States, the general public has been socialized to consider how people look (i.e. skin color, hair texture, facial features) to determine their *race* (Smedley, 2015). However with the expansion of scientific knowledge, it is now clear, that all human beings are 99.9% identical in their genetic makeup (NHGRI, 2015). Many scientists believe that differences in the remaining 0.1% of human DNA contain important clues that primarily hold the answers to the causes and cures of diseases. Scientists use that information to find better ways to improve health and prevent disease (NHGRI, 2015). A small fraction of the 0.1% of human DNA determines physical features (i.e. hair texture, facial features, skin color, etc.), which are characterized by ethnicity.

Ethnicity or **ethnic group** generally refers to a person (or group of people) physical features, nation/region of origin, customs, ways of being, and religion. (Markus, 2008). In research, the words ethnicity and race are often used interchangeably. Ethnicity can also be a source of meaning, action, and identity. It often gives a sense of belonging, pride, and motivation (Markus, 2008). In this book, the word ethnicity will be used instead of the word *race*. I'm writing these guidelines for discussing race with children, intentionally using the word *race* to only represent who we are as a human species. In doing so, the notion that all humans are created equally and should be treated as equals is promoted on both overt and covert levels, and intentionally on both the conscious and subconscious levels. Similarly, a definition of prejudice and discrimination is necessary.

Prejudice is prejudgment without knowledge. More specifically, it can be defined as beliefs or feelings that are negative toward individuals or groups, based only on their ethnic group, nationality (Raabe & Beelmann, 2011), religion, gender, socio-economic status, or sexual orientation. Prejudice reflects a generalization where the negative conclusion a person develops addresses most or all members of the ethnic group, discounting individual variances. (Raabe & Beelmann, 2011). Decisions made on prejudice, leads to discrimination.

Discrimination is manifested in two ways. Individual discrimination and institutional discrimination. Individual discrimination is direct, and involves overt actions, explicit discriminatory acts, or subtle micro-aggressions (Lemley, 2014). Racial jokes or comments are a form of discrimination that implicitly (or explicitly) persecutes historically marginalized people (Lemley, 2014).

Micro-aggressions are forms of discrimination. There are three types of micro-aggressions (Sue et. al., 2009). The first is often referred to as a **micro assault**. A micro assault is a verbal or nonverbal behavior that is meant to hurt the intended victim through name calling or avoidant behavior (Speicher, 2014). Using racial slurs, or moving to avoid interacting with someone from a group different from your own, would fall into this category. A micro insult is the second kind of micro-aggression.

A **micro insult** is a type of discrimination that, includes any communication that expresses insensitivity and demeans an individual's ethnic heritage. (Speicher, 2014). Micro insults are subtle and are often unintentional, as compared to micro assault. For example, if someone is talking to a person of color and suggests they got their job, promotion, or admission into a university based on a quota system rather than merit; or by ignoring contributions of a person of color in the classroom or in a group conversation (Speicher, 2014). The third type of micro-aggression is called a micro invalidation.

A **micro invalidation** is any communication that minimizes, excludes, negates, or nullifies the psychological thoughts, feelings, or experiences of a person of color (Sue et. al., 2009). Suggesting that someone's experiences, interpretations, or feelings are invalid or too sensitive, is a micro invalidation. Commenting to an Asian American on their "good" English, suggests that they should not be or aren't native speakers of English. Similarly, saying to an African American that you, "don't see color", is invalidating that person's experiences as a person of color by suggesting that their ethnicity hasn't affected their life. These micro-aggressions are forms of individual discrimination, however discrimination can also be found on an institutional level.

Institutional Discrimination is a web of institutional policies, structures, and practices that persistently generate benefits for certain ethnic groups, while creating disadvantages for historically marginalized populations (Lemley, 2014). The roots of institutional discrimination are practices and processes that are often difficult to identify, but usually include racial profiling and systems of hiring practices. Discrimination can take on many forms, and also manifest itself through the use of dehumanization.

Dehumanization is a psychological process a person uses to justify inhumane and unfair treatment of people of another ethnic group. Most often, this practice is used towards Black/African Americans, particularly towards African American Men. This process may be conscious or subconscious. It equates people to animals and rationalizes perceiving another person as less human (Haslam, 2006). In some situations, dehumanization serves to justify the exclusion of some ethnic groups from moral consideration: it suggests that some people are not worth helping or forgiving (Costello & Hodson, 2014). Put simply, dehumanizing an ethnic group leads to the acceptance of consistent negative treatment, evaluation of, and violence toward that ethnic group (Costello & Hodson, 2014).

Dehumanization can involve explicit animalistic comparisons, such as historical portrayals of people of African descent as monkeys or portrayals of people of Jewish descent as vermin (Livingstone- Smith, 2011). Although discrimination through dehumanization can take many forms, one of the most powerful ways we as parents can end discrimination and racism, is by being a great role model for our children.

CHAPTER 3
BE A POSITIVE ROLE MODEL
CHILDREN REPEAT WHAT THEY SEE AND HEAR

Understanding the formation of prejudice, stereotypes, and discrimination has been a topic of social psychology for a long time. For over 60 years, research from various countries around the world indicate that a child's prejudice and discriminatory practices come from what they have seen and heard from their parents (Degner & Dalege, 2013). Children are taught directly or indirectly how to treat, or mistreat other people. Two processes happen to transfer beliefs: direct transfer and indirect transfer (Degner & Dalege, 2013).

Direct transfer is a process of a child embracing their parents prejudices, from being directly exposed to their parents words, gestures, and beliefs (Allport, 1954). Similarly, children develop prejudice through their parents' creation of an atmosphere of intolerance, where prejudice forms in their children (Allport, 1954). As such, creating an environment of allowing belittling other ethnic groups, and social behaviors related to those groups, may encourage behavior most often referred to as "bullying", in American society. It is also discrimination. In order to avoid unwanted bullying and discriminatory behavior, parents should emphasize positive attributes of other ethnic groups, and demonstrate remorse and empathy when you say or do something inappropriate.

A child's ability to observe and imitate is a remarkable quality, and is referred to by scientists as **modeling** (Severe, 1997). With that in mind, as responsible parents, our goal is to find opportunities to be intentional with pointing out the good in other ethnic groups. Acknowledging academic scholarship, athleticism, and kind behavior in ethnic groups different from your own are essential to developing your child's cultural awareness and teaching them not to discriminate. In doing so, you teach your child to see the good/non-stereotypical qualities in others. You also demonstrate that acknowledging the good in other people is important. It is also imperative that we admit when we use an inappropriate comment, or make a mistake of another kind.

Admitting to our children that we have made a mistake is the foundation of teaching them to be responsible, and to own their mistakes. You can be a great example to your child 95% of the time, but children will catch you in the 5% that you mess up (Severe, 1997). Don't get defensive when your child catches you misspeaking or misbehaving. That's a valuable learning opportunity, and a perfect time to teach them about accepting responsibility for their behavior. I have had plenty of learning/teaching opportunities like this with my daughter Zoe.

In July of 2007, I participated in Rev. Al Sharpton's movement to bury the n-word. Although the use and understanding of the n-word is complex, we made it simple…just don't say it. My daughter Zoe was 3 at the time, and we simply said to her that the n-word was hurtful to many people and no one should use it. I thought it was responsible to teach her what the real word was, because we have had to ask other relatives and friends not to use the word around Zoe. In our home it was like using any other form of profanity. Like children do, Zoe remembered not to use the n-word, and she heard me say it one day.

The truth is, I had never stopped using the n-word. I just didn't use it in public or around my daughter. I used it often in my car, while navigating through the consistently horrendous traffic in Atlanta. Everyone who drove too slow, drove too fast, cut me off, or did anything I did not like, I called the n-word: gender, ethnic group, or age did not matter. One Friday after picking Zoe up from school, and hurrying through traffic (trying to make it to the West side of I-20 before traffic got too bad), someone cut me off. Then they slowed down and hit the brakes, like they were trying to cause an accident. I shouted, "Look at this n-word", and I meant it!

As children do, Zoe quickly realized I said a bad word. She scolded me, and asked, "Mommy, why would you say an ugly word like that"? I explained to her that I was frustrated, but wrong, and should not have used that word. I also explained that people say things when they are upset, that they wouldn't say if they weren't upset. This example is an illustration of why we must be intentional about eliminating certain words from our verbal lexicon and our consciousness. In doing so, when we get upset, awful things will not come out of our mouths.

Since that time, I have made a conscious effort to replace the n-word with another n-word…NUT! When I'm in traffic, whether I'm by myself or with others in the car, I try to keep my cool. However, on the rare occasion that I lose it, other people are called "nuts". As kids do, Zoe shared this embarrassing moment often, and told people that mommy said the n-word. I'm still embarrassed when she tells the story, but I own my mistake, and share what we both learned. I am mindful to model good behavior with my words and deeds. I am also mindful of not minimizing other people's pain and experiences based on my biases.

Our biases can cause us to further injure victims of racism or discrimination. By refusing to acknowledge the anger and anxiety-provoking nature of racism, we add to the trauma and paranoia that results from the initial experience (Williams, 2015). This often results in victims of racism and discrimination feeling as if they are "going crazy". Chronic fear of and anger from experiences of racism often leads to hyper-vigilance and paranoia, which are contributing factors to post traumatic stress disorder (PTSD) (Carter, 2007). As parents, we must recognize that trauma is real, and encourage our children to know with certainty to be empathetic to experiences other people have.

Racism still exists, therefore trauma from racism still exists. In a society where racism is deeply woven into the core of every aspect of social and governmental processes, we must admit that racism is perpetual. Racism is an ongoing, consistent, never-ending issue for most African American/Black people. African American people feel the effects of racism on a continuous basis, therefore the topic of racism is always a relevant topic. Is it unreasonable to use "post" in relation to racism and trauma experienced from racism, if racist experiences have never ended?

After considering the hundreds of ways and thousands of places where a racist experience can cause trauma, the term **Constant Traumatic Stress Disorder (CTSD)** is more a appropriate term (Andrews, 2016). I first heard the term used by Morehouse graduate and certified personal trainer, Glenn Andrews. Mr. Andrews explained how trauma shows up constantly in the body, and has to be addressed on a daily basis when working out and training the muscles to relieve that stress and trauma (Andrews, 2016). When we consider where that trauma and stress comes from, the underlying culprit for many scenarios is racism. Whether we consider traumatic effects of racism constant or post, we still must be mindful to deal with it as we would any other victim of violent assault.

Trauma experienced by rape victims and victims of racism are very similar (Bryant-Davis and Ocampo, 2005). Both are an assault on the personhood and integrity of the victim. Similar to rape victims, race-related trauma victims respond with shock, disbelief, or dissociation (Williams, 2013). This response, although it is a natural one, can prevent them from recovering in a healthy way. Victims of rape and racism often feel shame, and blame themselves because they did not defend themselves. This response often leads to low self-concept and self-destructive behaviors (Williams, 2013). The researchers in the study also drew a parallel between race-related trauma victims and victims of domestic violence. In both horrible acts, victims are often made to feel shame over allowing themselves to be victimized (Bryant-Davis & Ocampo, 2005).

For instance, people who experience discrimination or a racist incident are often told that if they are polite, work hard, and/or dress in a certain way, they will not encounter racism or discrimination (Williams, 2013). When these rules are followed and racism continues, then powerlessness, hyper vigilance, and other symptoms associated with PTSD (or CTSD) develop or get worse (Bryant-Davis & Ocampo, 2005). With these facts in mind, we must acknowledge the pain of other people and be compassionate. It is important that our children see us modeling empathy and an attitude that embraces and appreciates diversity.

CHAPTER 4
EMBRACE DIVERSITY
HIGHLIGHT THE POSITIVE IN OTHER ETHNIC GROUPS

By the time children start Kindergarten, they approve stereotypes and show prejudices based on ethnicity, age, attractiveness, disability status, and gender (Bigler & Wright, 2014). With that in mind, we should teach our kids early and intentionally about accepting other people, regardless of how they look. Waiting for a teachable moment, or for indications that our kids are ready to learn more, are not strategies that work for teaching diversity awareness and tolerance (Whittemore, 2009). Dr. Michael D. Baran, an anthropologist and cognitive psychologist at Harvard University, suggests that you should be intentional, but not direct, in teaching your children about ethnic diversity (Whittemore, 2009).

Being too direct without a clear explanation is, "an eat your vegetables" kind of approach (Whittemore, 2009). Sometimes telling kids what to do, ensures that they will do the opposite especially if you are not clear with explaining why you are giving them an instruction. Instead, give them the tools to understand our complicated social world, and the confidence to ask questions when they are confused (Whittemore, 2009).

Dr. Baran also suggests that age two or three is not too early to start a conversation about ethnic differences (Whittemore, 2009). **Parents can begin by trying new foods related to other cultures, and using that experience to explain differences. Again, this approach is intentional, but not direct.** You can also read books about children in other countries, and learn some simple words in a different language (Whittemore, 2009). Talk to your child about the world and all the different people in it. Present enough ideas to pique your child's curiosity and encourage them to think critically. As parents, guardians, and community members, we must answer their questions honestly and transparently.

Be prepared for the age-old question that my experiences as a teacher have taught me, White kids ask a lot, "Does Black skin rub off?". Parents must be prepared for other questions that may initially leave you taken aback. To prepare yourself, I suggest you use the workbook to help you recall your personal experiences and biases. It will also help you prepare appropriate answers before you talk to your children. I had to answer an equally difficult question, "Why are White people so mean?", after my daughter asked with genuine concern and contriteness during a PBS tv special on the Civil Rights Movement. She was 6 at the time.

After growing up in a racially hostile environment where I was often the only Black person in my class, I intentionally chose to shelter my child from the awful cruelties my sister and I endured as children. As an adult, I chose to live in a predominately African American county, in a predominately African American city, in a predominately African American neighborhood, and chose a school that was predominately African American for my daughter. I just knew that she would not experience racism on any level, at least not for a while. Like many parents, I avoided "the race talk" like the plague.

Now, I was faced with a question that I had previously mentioned briefly. I didn't know what to say, so I asked her if I could think about the answer and get back to her later. She said ok, and seemed to forget that she even asked the question. I sat quietly and prayed as she continued to watch tv. I asked God how I should answer the question. At that point, many questions came to me. No answers, only questions. Where else has Zoe seen White people? What experiences did she have with White people? What has she seen of White people? How would she know anything different from what she has seen? Have I taught her anything intentionally? What have I taught her, directly or indirectly? At that point, I realized that my child only knew about White people from what she saw in tv/movies and what she heard from experiences shared by me and other family members. Most of it was not good.

With that in mind, along with my commitment to teaching, seeing and believing the best in all people, I made sure she met the White people in my circle of friends. Although I had plenty of books about African American heritage and culture, I had few that included other cultures. The more I exposed Zoe to diverse cultures, the more my mind and heart expanded. I started to try to see good in other ethnic groups, and make sure she heard me verbalize those positive things. Being a good role model is the best way to make sure our children embrace and are exposed to diversity.

The academic research community suggests that the best way to reduce children's prejudices is to bring it up early, and to model an inclusive home (Tatum, 1999). Having an inclusive home demonstrates that you have friends and business associates from various backgrounds and ethnic groups. You are telling your children in a non-verbal way that being around people who are different from you is ok. It also helps children develop a mindset that having people around you who look different (from you), is "normal". Additionally, having a diverse representation of friends and associates humanizes ethnic groups that may be dehumanized in American culture. Although creating an atmosphere of acceptance is practical for some people, for other parents, demonstrating that norm and beginning that conversation with children can be difficult.

Dr. Beverly Tatum, former president of Spelman College, suggests that the awkwardness of relating to ethnic groups other than our own is due to a lack of direct, intentional communication from _our_ parents in many of our childhoods. Some parents are concerned about saying the wrong thing and "sounding racist", even if they have good intentions (Tatum, 1999). Naively, some parents believe that if they talk about issues of ethnic differences with their children, they will cause them to notice ethnicity or differences in a way that they did not before. That notion simply is not true. Parents of children from all ethnic backgrounds should discuss racism with their kids, if they want to raise children who are socially appropriate without a lot of biases (Pinola, 2015). Our duty as parents is also to ensure that our children can function in our interracial and global society. Silence on the matter doesn't prevent racism, it actually helps perpetuate prevalent prejudices, (Pinola, 2015). The more you discuss it, the more aware of appropriate responses you and your children become.

For some parents, the "race talk," is as difficult as the birds and the bees talk (Tatum, 1999). Other parents are forced into that awkward conversation with their children, after an experience with racism, discrimination or prejudice. As such, be mindful to be prepared, and be honest with yourself about your biases before you begin that conversation. Lecia Brooks, the director of the *Teaching Tolerance* program at The Southern Poverty Law Center, emphasizes that the discussion parents have with their children should be purposeful, beginning with certain goals in mind (Whittmore, 2009). Ms. Brooks also suggests that people tend to associate with others who they perceive to be like themselves, and who share their worldview. Often those people look the same ethnically and behave the same culturally. So it takes an intentional, sustained commitment to move away from comfortable, familiar habits and associate with people who we may perceive as different.

The Answers accompanying coloring book is a great place to begin this indirect, intentional conversation with 2-6 year olds. In kind, *The*

Answers playing cards are a good place to begin for 7-12 year olds. Conversations about TV shows your children watch, or local headlines from social media sites, are a great place to begin that intentional, indirect conversation with teenagers or young adults. Regardless of your ethnic background, seeing the positive attributes in others is important. However, you must also nurture a strong sense of identity for yourself and your family.

CHAPTER 5
DEVELOP A STRONG SENSE OF SELF-IDENTITY
HOW DO YOU DEFINE YOURSELF & YOUR ETHNICITY?

Self-identity is the way a person defines her or himself, and how a person differentiates themselves from other people (De Cremer & Tyler, 2005). A person's ability to develop a clear definition of self is associated with the ability to: 1) effectively manage stress, 2) have balance between emotional connection and independence in intimate relationships, and 3) differentiate between their thoughts and feelings (Gushue et al., 2013). **Differentiated self-identity** is seeing yourself in many different ways: ex., a mother, a wife, a child, a friend, a student, etc. Differentiation of self-identity also includes a person who may view her or himself as a leader in professional settings, and a follower in other social settings. They may be the "life of the party" with their friends, but may be more reserved in settings with their parents and siblings. An individual's ability to recognize a variety of ethnic and cultural perspectives (including complex ethnic and gender identity statuses) requires a differentiated self-identity (Gushue et al., 2013). This type of self-identity is open to multiple points of view, and does not overreact to others people's assumptions and values. The construct of differentiation of self is understood as a form of psychological maturity in the areas of family and social relationships.

The definition of self-identity (that people develop and embrace for themselves), has huge implications for how they evaluate justice and respond to fairness-related events. Research indicates the effects of fairness on attitudes and behaviors are weakened by self-identity, so justice has stronger effects when it is consistent with a person's self-identity (Brockner, De Cremer, Van den Bos, & Chen, 2005; Johnson, Selenta, & Lord, 2006). In other words, if it serves the purposes of who you are and how you see yourself, then fairness is achieved (from your perspective). It's all about perspective. Self-identity may also reconcile justice-based effects on attitudes and behaviors (Lind, 2001; Tyler & Blader, 2003).

For example, fairness communicates to people that they are valued and respected. In turn, the value a person places on the ethnic group they identify with, also increases if they perceive that group is treated fairly (De Cremer, Tyler, & den Ouden, 2005; Olkkonen & Lipponen, 2006). As a result, their cooperation in working with their ethnic group and other ethnic groups also increases. Understanding the effects that justice has on self-identity, sheds light on one of the ways through which justice-related identity is translated into behavior (Johnson & Lord, 2010).

Research also verifies that justice affects self-identity activation on an explicit and implicit level. It balances the effects of justice on trust, cooperation, and counterproductive behavior (Johnson & Lord, 2010). The construct of a person's self-identity is directly impacted by how justly they believe they have been treated, and is an indication of psychological maturity. Similarly, ethnic identity is a series of self-identity distinctions that evolve and change over time. **Ethnic identity** describes the emotional, cognitive and behavioral processes which influence how a person interprets and responds to "racial stimuli" in the social environment (Helms, 1995).

Ethnic identity is how a person defines her or himself based on commonalities with other people a person identifies with. These commonalities include: physical appearance, language, customs, religion, history, nation/region of origin, ways of being, names, physical appearance, and/or genealogy or ancestry (Markus, 2008).

Research indicates that people who have a more mature sense of ethnic identity have healthier and more developed psychological functioning (Buckley & Carter, 2005; Nghe & Mahalik, 2001). Put simply, if you can see yourself in several different ways, from several different perspectives, you are more likely to be able to accept people who are different from you. Whether those differences are based on physical appearances, religion, or socio-economic status, differentiation of self helps you develop a sense of empathy. Seeing yourself in different ways gives you a variety of perspectives to use to be able to relate to others.

Keep in mind that your primary identity as a human should be emphasized with your children. As humans, there are certain undeniable scientific facts that transpire when we communicate. At the moment we make contact with other people, biochemical reactions are triggered at every level of our bodies (Glaser, 2014). Our heart responds in two ways — electrochemical and chemical. When we interact with others we have a biochemical or neurochemical response to the interaction. We also receive electrical signals from others during that interaction. As our bodies read and process another person's energy (which we pick up within 10 feet of the person) the process of connecting or rejecting begins (Glaser, 2014).

Chapter 5 in the workbook includes several questions and resources to assist you in determining your self-identity, and differentiating your self identity. Regardless of how you identity yourself, I encourage you to take some time and complete the workbook activity.

Troya Bishop, M. Ed.

CHAPTER 6
EMBRACE FAMILY HISTORY:
ACCENTUATE THE POSITIVE

In 2006, Dr. Henry Louis Gates made the search for roots and meanings of lineage quite popular in America with his PBS project, *African American Lives*. In 2007 both the Black and White descendants of the landmark Plessy v. Ferguson case met in New Orleans to discuss the past and present significance of their ancestors' lives (Parham, 2008). That study and other research projects like it, reveal that the process of engaging in family history discovery as a collective family unit, provides a foundation for those who participate to better understand other ethnic groups. Research also indicates that there is a need to recognize the public significance of these private histories (Parham, 2008).

In doing so, healing racism and discrimination can begin on the local and community levels. In each city across America, there are events that took place that shaped that community. Having a discussion about who your family is, and how they have shaped the community, city, county, or state where you reside can provide your children with a huge sense of pride and ownership, regarding moving the community forward. Naturally, different people in a community will remember events from the past in different ways.

Our memory is affected by our social environment (Zerubavel, 1996). The influence of our family members on the way we "remember" a past that we have not lived through is a basic part of our **mnemonic socialization**; which is the way we learn to remember and interpret the past (Zerubavel, 1996). This socialization begins within the family and we gradually apply or revise what we have learned as we venture out into the community and the world at large. With this in mind, we must find the positive things our family members accomplished; accomplishments of individual family members or accomplishments that are shared collectively.

Since families in the U.S. are often ethnically homogeneous, our mnemonic socialization is also shaped by our ethnic group membership (Parham, 1996). Therefore it is not surprising, that there are distinct approaches to social memory construction in the United States that vary by ethnic group. But when this uniqueness is linked to unequal power, then private family narratives may be transformed into inequities in public representations of the past.

Those inequities provide opportunities for community discussion and healing. If those opportunities are recognized by community members of all ethnic groups, healing on the local level can certainly begin.

Again, I want to emphasize the need to tell the truth about the past, even if it is difficult. In kind, I want to emphasize the need to find family members that contributed in a positive way to society. This will keep the perspective geared toward healing and moving the family forward with a new perspective and a commitment to a brighter future. I learned the importance of focusing on a positive perspective while I was a middle school teacher.

At the time, I was teaching World Studies to 7th grade students in one of the most ethnically diverse schools in the state of Georgia (Dekalb, 2015). Like most teachers, I connected poignant parts of each standard I taught in the month of February to the Civil Rights Movement. I also enjoyed introducing my students to important people and voices from the civil rights era that they were not familiar with.

Since I was teaching in the Metro Atlanta area, I made sure that my Civil Rights heroes were also local, and major contributors to Metro Atlanta as well. The look on their faces when they "met" people like C.T. Vivian, Ralph McGill, Andrew Young, and Joel Chandler Harris, were priceless. I made sure that we explored a different perspective:

one of students, writers, Black people, White people, etc. A perspective that included critical thinking about the pieces of the collective puzzle of humanity.

This perspective kept my students engaged and fascinated. Assignments which required them to think critically about who is well known from the Civil Rights movement, who is not, and the possible reasons why, was an assignment they enjoyed. That made my life easier as their teacher, and their life in social studies class more interesting. Exploring a different perspective is what discovering your family history will give to your children as well. One of the best ways to engage them in that process, is through critical thinking.

CHAPTER 7
ENCOURAGE CURIOSITY
TEACH AND DEMONSTRATE CRITICAL THINKING

Critical thinking is a person's ability to assess data or information and decide how the information should be used based on how accurate it is (Price-Mitchell, 2015). In order to develop critical thinking skills, an individual must be curious, open-minded and willing to consider alternative ways of looking at solutions. Most children naturally possess those qualities. Kids are inquisitive, so consistently encouraging their curiosity should not be difficult. As children grow into pre-adolescents and teenagers, their critical thinking skills will help them make judgments independently of parents (Price-Mitchell, 2015), which is the ultimate goal for most parents.

To be good at thinking, children must believe that thinking is fun and *want* to be good at it. Good thinkers practice thinking just like they practice basketball or soccer (Price-Mitchell, 2015). We must encourage our children to practice thinking often, from an early age.

Young children can understand critical thinking, and will automatically apply it when they believe it benefits them. Consider how many times you have heard your child say, "that's not fair", or "that's not nice", or something of that nature. When children believe something is unfair, they know and are able to boldly articulate it. It is at times like this, that you can teach your child to use critical thinking. You can also teach them to think critically about the basics of human cruelties like slavery and bullying (Tatum, 1999).

Dr. Beverly Tatum suggests that any parent can explain slavery (or segregation) for their child and encourage curiosity by using this example and asking follow-up questions: Slavery happened a long time ago, and holding people captive and making them work without paying them is unfair. She also suggests that parents can further explain to their children that slavery ended, because many people thought it was unfair and worked to change it. Dr. Tatum continues to encourage parents to emphasize that no ethnic group is all bad or all good. Asking your child questions about the difference in how "good people" and "bad people" behave is a good place to start teaching critical thinking. Dr. Tatum also suggests using this example: in the U.S., some White people were slave owners, but some White people also worked against slavery. Black people were enslaved, but many resisted their mistreatment by running away and helping others escape. Offering your children examples of people on both sides of any issue fosters critical thinking skills and encourages them to embrace diversity and enhances their ability to appreciate other perspectives. Unfortunately, our own biases and prejudices often keep us as parents from presenting alternate perspectives.

Our biases also make us (as parents and guardians) more likely to ask our children questions at the remembering level, which according to Bloom's Taxonomy is the lowest level of thinking (Garland, 2014). This includes questions like: who, what, where, when, and why. These types of questions only require our children to use memorization, not higher level thinking, to respond to the questions. As parents, we want to encourage our children to think for themselves, and groom them to be leaders and to avoid peer pressure. We want them to have the skills to effectively analyze, listen, and interpret information that will affect their lives and the lives of those around them (Garland, 2014). After the remembering and understanding levels of Bloom's taxonomy, the next four levels are higher levels of thinking that we want to encourage our children to develop.

The last four stages are: applying, analyzing, evaluating and creating. In the applying stage, children are asked to use a concept in a new situation and apply what they know. A parent could ask their child how they would solve a given real-life situation (Garland, 2014). Or, a parent may also ask why something is significant, or ask their child to predict what will happen next in a given situation (McBin, 2011). After asking several higher level Bloom's Taxonomy questions, during various conversations, you will get a feel of your child's ability to think critically. Be patient and give your child extra time to respond. If your child is not used to higher level questioning or using their brain for this type of thinking, it may take some time for them to process the information and be able to respond. With practice, higher level questioning will become easier for you and your child.

For more ideas on how to teach your child critical thinking skills and for fun activities to do with your children that require higher level thinking, use the companion workbook (Chapter 7).

IMPLICATIONS
WHAT DOES IT ALL MEAN? HOW DOES IT EFFECT ME?

There are two crucial implications that may take place when racism in our society is not addressed with our children. The first implication is psychological in nature. The fact is, racism is real. It is painful, and it is perpetual. Being able to recognize it, and empathize with those who have historically suffered the trauma and effects of racism is crucial to raising a psychologically healthy child. It is also important to acknowledge that due to the institutional nature of racism, most African American people, still feel the effects of racism on a regular basis. Although people of color from various ethnic groups feel the painful effects of racism, research shows that Blacks face racism more often, and in a more direct way, yielding more psychologically damaging results (Helms, Nicholas, and Green, 2012). Ignoring racism and refusing to recognize it for what it is may result in you or your child becoming a **narcissist**, or having a disorder related to narcissism.

According to the journal *Psychology Today*, narcissism and Narcissistic Personality Disorder (NPD) involves a lack of empathy for other people, and a deep need for admiration from all people around them (2015). People who are narcissistic are usually described as demanding, self-centered, and manipulative. Narcissism also involves selfishness, and manipulation that is frequently related to getting and maintaining power (*Psychology Today*, 2015). Clinical psychologist, Dr. Eileen Kennedy-Moore, suggests that narcissism is a disorder of relationships (2015). Equally, racism is a disorder of relationships.

Dr. Kennedy-Moore also explains, that at about seven years old, children become able to compare themselves realistically to their peers (2015). For most children, this leads to a drop in overall self-esteem, but for others it can be the beginning of a narcissistic view of themselves. Narcissism is not only believing, "I am great!". It is having a deep rooted knowing and belief of superiority. Racism also has a deep rooted knowing and belief of superiority. Narcissism believes, "I am better and more important than you!" (Kennedy-Moore, 2015). Racism also believes, "I am better and more important than you!" Narcissists always want to be the center of attention. Racists also want to be the center of attention. Narcissists have trouble putting themselves in other people's shoes (Kennedy-Moore, 2015). Racists also have trouble putting themselves in other people's shoes. Although they may brag and seem confident, their self-esteem is actually fragile and they will act aggressively if they feel criticized or rejected in any way (Kennedy-Moore, 2015). Be sure to complete the workbook activity for this chapter to get strategies to use to raise a healthy child, and avoid having a narcissistic or otherwise psychologically unhealthy child. Although there are many steps we can take as parents to raise healthy children, our culture breeds individuality and nurtures narcissism (Plante, 2013).

According to research recently published in the *Journal of Personality and Social Psychology*, both American citizens and non-American people perceive other Americans as being extremely narcissistic (Miller et. al., 2015). The problem in our very individualistic, American society is the plethora of messages that reinforce the narcissistic notion that, "it's all about you" (Plante, 2013). The findings of this in-depth study also reflects the belief that the average American is grandiose, self-centered, and callous (Miller et. al., 2015). Although an inflated view of narcissism of a typical member of a person's culture is shared across a diverse set of regions and cultures, the effects are generally smaller in other regions of the world. Ironically, those other regions of the world have far more people per capita than the United States, making the severity of the disorder of narcissism even more prevalent. With this in mind, the mental health of our children and of other children should be paramount.

The American Psychological Association suggests that Mental and behavioral health is a critical and frequently unaddressed matter in racial and ethnic minority communities. The lack of attention to the mental and behavioral health needs of ethnic minorities and the inadequate provision of culturally and linguistically appropriate mental health care in these minority communities demonstrates a clear need for encouraging collaboration and finding ways to close the gap in care (APA, 2015). The federal government has a critical role to play in addressing the issue of ethnic disparities in mental health status and mental health care by supporting legislation and regulations that will improve the health and well-being of minorities. (APA, 2015). We as parents also hold that same responsibility.

Not addressing racism with your children, and learning about this societal ill for yourself may also lead to you or your children being labeled as racist. Bryant-Davis and Ocampo noted similar courses of psychopathology between rape victims and victims of racism in their 2005 study (Williams, 2013). Both events are an assault on the personhood and integrity of the victim. Similar to rape victims, race-related trauma victims may respond with disbelief, shock, or dissociation, which can prevent them from responding to the incident in a healthy manner. The victim may then feel shame and self-blame because they were not able to respond or defend themselves, which may lead to low self-concept and self-destructive behaviors. In the same study, a parallel was drawn between race-related trauma victims and victims of domestic violence. Both survivors are made to feel shame for allowing themselves to be victimized. For instance, someone who may have experienced a racist incident may be told that if they are polite, work hard, and/or dress in a certain way, they will not encounter racism. When these rules are followed yet racism persists, powerlessness, hyper vigilance, and other symptoms associated with PTSD may develop or worsen (Bryant-Davis & Ocampo, 2005).

For example, when unarmed Black people are murdered, it is widely suggested that the unarmed victim should have done something different. Dressed different, spoken different, presented themselves different. Those suggestions are cruel, painful, and further victimizing to the person of the offense, the victim's family, and many community members as well. However, what appears to the untrained eye to be anger and flippantness, is medically considered as effects of PTSD.

Again, to help your children avoid the racist mindset that leads to the statements and actions mentioned above, we as parents must act intentionally. Questions that help reveal biases and encourage critical thinking on this issue are included in the workbook. Be sure to complete that section with your children.

CONCLUSION
HOW DO WE MOVE FORWARD?

The consistent lack of understanding in the United States about how people respond to poverty and oppression globally, has contributed to the overall dehumanization of Black and Brown people around the world, especially African Americans. Parents of all ethnic backgrounds must be intentional with teaching their children about the humanity of African American people, to ensure that they perceive and value Black and Brown people as human beings. The use of appropriate vocabulary is absolutely necessary, when discussing racism with children. Parents should also be more aware and intentional with the behavior they are modeling, because your children are watching and will duplicate the behavior parents and guardians display.

Racism-related experiences can range from frequent micro-aggressions to blatant hate crimes and physical assault (Williams, 2015). Micro-aggressions are pervasive acts of racism; they can be vague insults or non-verbal exchanges, such as a scowl or refusal to sit next to a Black person in a meeting or on public transportation. During micro-aggressions, the victim loses key mental and emotional capacity trying to understand the intention of the perpetrator (Williams, 2015). Keeping in mind the institutional and often direct and interpersonal nature of racism, all society members must acknowledge that these events happen frequently, making it difficult for many African Americans to mentally and emotionally manage the volume of racial stressors. We as guardians, parents and community members should demonstrate a sympathetic response to pain and hurt, whether we encounter it in the media or in person.

Our behavior must model and reflect genuine concern, and not dismissiveness. We must encourage our children and others to see the beauty and differences in others. If you choose to be colorblind, and promote colorblindness in your children, you teach them not to appreciate the uniqueness in people who are different from them. We are different in appearance, and being different is great. We must remind our children that there is only one race: the human race.

Zig Ziglar, an American author, salesman, and motivational speaker reminds us in his book, *The Answer to Racism,* that even the Bible does not use the word race in referring to people. Instead, it describes all human beings as being of "one blood" in Acts 17:26 (Zigler, 2015). This further emphasizes that we are all related and all humans are descendants of the first man and woman. With this in mind, we must make a collective effort to walk in unity.

Dr. Tony Evans, the first African American to earn a doctoral degree from Dallas Theological Seminary, reminds us that unity does not equal sameness (1995). People from different cultures, religions, and ethnic groups can have unity, without being the same or believing the same things. Unity is a requirement for healthy families and communities. Unity is also a requirement for a healthy marriage, although the husband and wife are different physically, and in their personality and temperament (Evans, 1995), God still requires them to walk in unity. Unity requires oneness of purpose. That means, all parties are willing to move forward in a positive direction for the common good of all involved (Evans, 1995). Of course, unity is simple, but not easy. Unwillingness to consider the other person and walk in unity is the reason behind the hostility in our culture, and the reason for the increasing amounts of failed marriages. However, when people refuse to cooperate with efforts of progress and unity, we must hold them accountable (Evans, 1995).

All community members, parents and those without children should speak up and speak out when they see wrong doing. The visible leadership of the Christian church cannot condone public rejection of people who are different (Evans, 1995). There is no more time for us to sit by passively and wait for people to change. People must be willing to learn and remain committed to the process of life-long learning; that cannot be done without the knowledge that they will be held accountable for how they treat other members of God's family (Evans, 1995).

One of the most poignant teachings regarding truth, culture, and unity is in John 4, when Jesus Christ encountered a woman from Samaria. This story provides outstanding principles for people of different faiths and different ethnic backgrounds that are needed to establish unity (Evans, 1995). Ultimately, we as parents must be careful of what we say and the way we say it.

Words are powerful. We must be sure to model appropriate vocabulary and to use words in their proper context. Our children are watching, and they will see and say everything we model. World renowned poet, actress, singer, and five time Grammy winner, Dr. Maya Angelou, stresses that, "Words are 'things'. You must be careful about the words you use, or the words you allow to be used in your house… Words are things. You must be careful. Careful about calling people out of their names. Using racial partitives, and sexual partitives, and all of that ignorance. Don't do that. Someday we will be able to measure the power of words. I think they are things. I think they get on your wall. They get in your wall paper, and in your rugs. They get in your upholstery and in your clothes, and finally, they get into you." (Angelou, 2011). As we protect what goes into our minds and out of our mouths, we must be careful to behave as we want our children to behave: as compassionate, loving, fair people.

As we want understanding and empathy from other people, we must find it in ourselves to give it to other people, all people. Dr. Angelou also explained, "I have had so many rainbows in my clouds, and I've had a lot of clouds. But I have had so many rainbows…The thing to do it seems to me, is to prepare yourself so that you can be a rainbow in somebody else's cloud. Somebody who may not look like you, or may not call God the same name you call God, if they call God at all… They may not eat the same dishes prepared the way you do. They may not dance your dances, or speak your language, but be a blessing to somebody." (Angelou, 2011). Taking this step is the key to embracing diversity.

Changing the way you think, and being willing to make decisions to have a lifestyle which includes people from other ethnic groups is essential. Again, our children will listen to us and follow us when they know we are being authentic. According to Dr. Marshall Goldsmith, author of *Triggers: Creating Behavior that Lasts- Becoming the Person You Want to Be*, there are two immutable truths of behavioral change: 1) Meaningful behavioral change can be difficult to accomplish, and 2) No one can make an adult change against their will (2015). Behavioral change can be difficult to achieve as adults, because we often reason our way into excuses that negate our need for change. There is a difference between motivation, understanding and ability. Positive, consistent, behavioral change is challenging because we are attempting to change in an environment that is full of triggers (Goldsmith, 2015).

Those triggers may easily pull and push us off course. Fortunately, achieving meaningful and sustained change can be reached if we change what we believe (Goldsmith, 2015). The roots of what we believe is the driving force for our behavior. We must educate ourselves, and reinforce our critical thinking skills. We must question what we allow ourselves to believe, and allow our children see us in this process. Don't resist the need to change your behavior. There is always room for improvement.

I accept the challenge and opportunity to learn and grow daily. I am committed to being a better human being every day. I acknowledge, that although I am educated and compassionate to all people, the trauma that I have endured from many racist and discriminatory events in my life still effect what I say when I am in stressful situations, just as Dr. Marshall and the other doctors previously referenced have suggested. The residue from trauma rises, as the research studies mentioned earlier in this book suggested they would. As luck would have it, there were people there to witness my most recent incident.

I was traveling to a meeting with fellow activists. We decided to carpool. This time, I opted to be a passenger and not drive, because traffic is one of my triggers. As often happens in Atlanta traffic, a guy in a sports car sped up when he noticed that my friend had her signal on so we could merge into traffic. Although the other car sped up, the thick traffic caused that car to slow down enough so that my friend could make eye-contact. She motioned to him, and asked him if we could get over. He mouthed, "F**K YOU," gave the middle finger, and went fast enough to make sure that we could not merge. Without thinking, I shouted, "Now see, that's why I don't fool with White people".

A hush fell over the car. I felt all eyes on me, and I remembered that I was with my White friends. Yes, I was the only Black person in the car! Everyone started laughing hysterically, and quickly charged the foolish words that I used to my head and not to my heart. I apologized, but it fell on deaf ears…literally. They were still laughing at me. That incident continues to be a running joke in my circle of activist friends, which includes people of all faiths and all ethnic groups.

My hope is that we can all be as gracious as my friends were, and honest about mistakes we make. We have to reject the notion that we do not need to grow and change. Although I am well read, and have researched more on the topic of racism than most people I know, I still have plenty of room to grow and be compassionate to other people who are also in the process of growing. Often, it is easier to attack the strategy of the person who's trying to help than to try to solve the problem (Marshall, 2015). We as humans often fall back on a set of beliefs that trigger denial, resistance and ultimately self-delusion. They sabotage lasting change by canceling its possibility (Marshall, 2015). We employ these beliefs as articles of faith to justify our inaction and then wish away the result. These are called belief triggers. The workbook will help you identify and work through your belief triggers, so you will not pass them on to your children.

This mentality of reconciliation of words and deeds will help us talk to our children about racism, and hopefully help to end racism.

Troya Bishop, M. Ed.

THE CONVERSATION
AFRICAN AMERICAN MEN DISCUSS RACISM

Have you ever wanted to be a fly-on-the-wall and listen to African American men discuss racism? Now you can. I posed a few questions to African American men that I know, respect, and love. These are people I look up to, and often seek advice from. They are pillars in the community, and take their responsibility as men and protectors seriously. These men spend time building their families, and mentoring young men in their community. If you don't know any African American men personally, here are some of God's BEST, so check them out online when you can.

I was often confused with why people thought that Black men were bad, or dangerous. My experiences taught me that Black men are my friends and defenders. However, I now understand other people's experiences with Black men were limited to only what they receive in the media. The power and danger of media, and the one-sided perspective of Black people is constantly streaming on several stations (that everyone does not have the opportunity to experience the greatness of African American men, or to be exposed to the *idea* that they are great. How unfortunate. Those people who are sheltered in that way, are missing out on some of the most loyal, most loving beings on the planet. For that reason, I am honoring Black Men, through the poetry and song of one of my favorite R&B singers, Angie Stone.

Although the song, "Brotha" was recorded over 14 years ago, Angie Stone explained earlier this year on the Rickey Smiley Morning Show that the song is even more relevant now, when police brutality is highly publicized (Smiley, 2015). This year, she re-recorded the video, and featured some of the families affected by police violence. My hope and prayer is that people will see Black men as human. The dehumanization must stop, and we must honor all life. Black men are certainly worthy of honor.

Brotha
Angie Stone

He is my King, He is my one,
Yes he's my father, Yes he's my son.
I can talk to him because he understands,
Everything I go through ,and everything I am.
That's my support system. I can't live without him.

The best thing since sliced bread…
Is his kiss, his hugs, his lips, his touch
And I want the whole world to know, about my…

Black Brotha, I love ya, I will never try to hurt ya.
I want ya to know that I'm here for you - forever true.
Black Brotha, strong Brotha, there is no - one above ya
I want ya, to know that, I'm here for you - forever true

Quincy Allen – Air Force Master Sergeant, ret. & Security Guard

What did you teach your children about racism?

I taught more of a situational awareness or avoidance approach. I did not want them to take racist experiences head on, as those situations tend to be volatile, and unpredictable in nature. I wasn't ready to put them in "freedom fighter" status, or allow them to try civil disobedience. Eventually I will, but not yet!

For example I tried to keep them out of certain situations as much as I could, because we lived in a predominately White community rooted with racial tension. Often, as Black kids in our neighborhood gathered together: talking, laughing, and hanging out, the group would get large (more than 4 kids) after a little while. I saw the ensuing potential "situation" and would explain to them what I saw, and why I felt I had to do something.

I invited them all inside to hangout: to avoid a mischaracterization of Black-teenagers-having-fun, as "suspicious behavior" or as them doing something wrong. I have seen that mischaracterization happen quite frequently, when so called "large" groups of Black or minority teens get together. It is often seen as "gang activity", or trouble in some White communities. Those uninformed community members will call the police, and the police will harass the kids to get them to leave or break up the group. These encounters turn bad in a hurry, people get hurt, and lives are ruined. This was why I took more of a situational awareness and avoidance approach as often as possible, to protect my kids from dangers that racism can bring.

Quincy's family: grandfather, his son Quincy II, 22 years old and his daughter Shanell, 20 years old.

Barry Brown – Educator, Author, & Entrepreneur

What do you teach your kids about race and racism?

I teach my kids the "Golden Rule". Do unto others as you would have them do unto you. I share with them that our history in this country is not a pretty one. We as African Americans have gone through tremendous adversity in the United States, but we are still here and progressing because of our great ancestors that sacrificed their lives to allow us to live the way we live today!

My parents (their grandparents) were very active participants in the Civil Rights Movement of the 1960's via, "The Student Movement." I share with them that racism still exists, but that we focus on God, our family, our education and our business/work. "Knowledge makes a man unfit to be a slave." - Frederick Douglass

Have you had a racist incident that shaped you or your thoughts on racism?

Being stopped by the police this the worst experience. I hate being targeted because of how I look. I graduated from high school with honors, went to college on a football scholarship, earned a Bachelor's degree in English, started my own business, and started a family. But people can't see that when they look at me. I have been stopped by the police for DWB, "driving while Black", more than six (6) times in my life. They just see that you're Black and think you're a criminal. I have also had Caucasian men and women actually walk off the sidewalk (as we were approaching each other), and then they came back on the sidewalk after we passed each other. As if they were afraid of **me**! I have plenty more examples, but I digress. One Love!

How have you overcome racism?
I have not overcome racism, and I believe no one ever actually does overcome racism. We have amazing examples of how racism still exists and most likely will always exist, like the way President Obama is treated by other politicians and the media. No President in the history of the United States has faced the outright racism, blatant disrespect and hateful opposition that he has faced. God has blessed President Obama with the fortitude to push forward and still make great contributions to this country! He is a perfect example of how hard work and fortitude outshine the evils of racism.

Barry and his daughters: Aubri is 4 years old and Amari is 12 years old. He says they are his joy, and a huge part of why he is determined to continue to strive for greatness.

For more information about Barry Brown, visit:

HTTP://WWW.BREG1994.COM

Ron Allen – Political Activist for Social, Labor & Human Rights

What do you teach your kids about race and racism?

I have taught my children that all ethnic groups are equal. No ethnicity is better than yours and your ethnicity is no better than another. When I asked my daughters what I taught them about racism, Veronica replied, "Racism is unfair because you have to treat people the way you want to be treated. Most people want to be treated fair and with respect." That response made me proud. I'm honored God chose me to be their dad.

Ron teaching his children 13, and Veronica 11 about the importance of voting. Tweet Ron: @RonAllen247

Mawuli Davis – Attorney

How did you discuss racism with your children?

Before I had children, I was forced to reflect on how I would discuss race with my unborn sons. I was an officer in the Navy stationed in Spain, when a pregnant shipmate told us that when she had her child she was not going to teach her about race or racism. I reflected on her statement and I immediately became afraid for her unborn child. I thought that her not teaching her child about race was like not teaching her child about her family's history. Her child would not know what people of African descent had both created and overcome. It is a form of "historical amnesia" and amnesia is dangerous because you don't know who you are or where you are going; you are lost.

I then thought that to not tell her child about racism was like not telling her child about the dangers of fire, or drinking and driving, or playing with guns. To not provide her child with such basic but critical information would be to leave her vulnerable to the dangers of racism without any defenses. Since having sons, I have tried to teach them to be proud to be men of African descent, and aware of the system of institutional racism and white supremacy. Knowing who they are and understanding the system that continues to play a role in dehumanizing and endangering their very being will be a major factor in what they accomplish in their lives.

Mawuli Mel Davis is an "activist attorney" who practices civil rights law at the Davis Bozeman Law Firm and has organized to end institutional racism including attending the United Nations World Conference Against Racism in Durban, South Africa.

Mawuli with his sons. For more information about Mawuli's law practice visit: www.davisbozeman.com

John Fowler – Home Builder & Land Developer

What will you teach your daughters about racism?

I will let them know that racism does exist. Therefore, their mother and I considered what names we wanted our children to have. What's more important is that I want you girls to understand that you should never allow anyone to make you feel bad about being African American. Just Remember God made you as well as them. Just know that life is going to be hard but she who wants to win can. I want you girls to love and have respect for mankind. Dad does not want you girls focusing on the negativity of human nature. Know that when you put something into the universe, it will come back just like a boomerang. Always remember your mother and I are crawling so that you lovely girls can walk and your children can run and their children can fly. Stay focused on the positive aspect of life and remember racism does exist but you do not have to participate.

Proud father, John and his daughters Morgan and Madelyn.

Corneilus George – Educator & Comedian

What do you teach your kids about racism?

Teaching children about race and racism is a very difficult task, yet a very necessary one. The hard part for me, is that I understand that my children have not had the same life experiences with racism that I have. My children are growing up in a society where interracial dating will not get you a second look. People where we live accept it as a norm. To put it in context, imagine the looks some transgender couples may get now (people will stare, but be silent). I try to teach my children about racism as the topic, or situations as they arise, because in some cases it is a matter of life and death. With the current climate of police brutality (we know not all cops are bad), I make sure he understands how to remain calm and handle difficult situations in a peaceful manner. I had to explain to him that everyone is not going to see him as a nice gentle giant; and that some will see him as one of many of the bad images of Black men they see on TV.

I use movies and history to teach my children about race and racism. In the past I always pointed out to my son, "Why did the bad character have to be Black or Brown toned and the good pure one have to be White? Why are most of the super heroes White"? I do not bring this up to be prejudiced or discriminatory, but to make him aware of some of the images that are being portrayed. While watching his favorite movie "How to Train a Dragon 2", he noticed that the hero was a black dragon and he screamed, "See Dad, there are some good images of people of color"! I love my kids. They make me proud every day.

Tweet Corneilus: @jcorneliusg1

Harvey Holmes – Retired U.S. Coast Guard & Security Manager

What did you teach your kids about racism?

Before I taught my kids anything, I listened to my father. My father taught me that I am just as good or as bad as anyone else. I taught my sons that they were able to be whatever they wanted be as long as they prepared themselves for it. I emphasized to them that they are not inferior to anyone. They both had a diverse group of friends. They looked at me and the group of people that I served with (in the Coast Guard): how we worked together, lived in the same neighborhood, looked out for each other, and looked out for each other's families. I had to learn excerpts from the March on Washington speech in high school, so I taught them to judge a person not by the color of their skin, but by the content of their character. My oldest son, Timothy, had the same friends from first grade until college. When he left this earth, they showed their love. That made me very proud. Vincent learned that not all of his friends were of good character. Now that he is a father, he truly understands.

Harvey is a father and grandfather who is active and constantly learning and guiding future generations. He is an avid outdoorsman and loves to grow the minds of others.

Solomon Muhammad – Police Officer; U.S. Marine ret.

What do you teach your daughter about racism?

Teaching my daughter about racism can be a very difficult task. I'm a Marine Veteran and Police Officer Of 19 years. Racism is a conversation that many will avoid, but as a Black man, there's no way around it. I can remember being in high school in Mississippi: White students would sit in one section and Black students would sit all over. It was clear that there was a great divide. I have (on many occasions) taught my daughter about the south and its violent history, especially Emmitt Till and many others that are unknown. As her father and protector, it's my duty and my honor to make sure she knows what she needs to know.

I feel as a father I cannot just *say* racism is wrong, but I must explain *why* it's wrong, and what it all means. As a child, I had a White friend across the railroad tracks in my rural community. We would play together, and go muddying together (ridding a truck in the mud). My parents told me his father rode around with a Rebel flag and was part of the Klan (KKK). They were afraid for me to continue to be friends with him, because of violent, racially motivated acts of hate that happened to Black people in our area. I later stopped going muddying with him. I have to be honest with my daughter about the harsh realities, so she will understand more about me, our family, and the history of the Black struggle in America.

Once I joined The USMC, I began to see the more covert and overt institutional operations of White supremacy and racism. I worked as an administrative clerk and coached Marines to shoot rifles and pistols. In the office, I observed race based issues, and radical racism in the fleet on the job issues. The racism was brutal, but I survived. I'm proud to be able to teach my daughter how to thrive, not just survive, in the face of racism.

Omar Howard – Professional Mentor & Life Coach for Young Men

What do you teach your children about racism?

I teach my sons that racism is very real. Some people see your Black skin, and are automatically afraid. We as Black men have to work twice as hard for what most other people take for granted. Some people call that the, "Black Tax", and those of us who pay it know exactly what it is.

I took my sons and my mentees to the MLK Jr, Center in Atlanta to teach them about the history of Black people in America, how much we endured, and how many leaders were willing to take a stand for what was right. They don't get the chance to see positive Black men often, especially not on tv, so I felt like I had to take them.

Most importantly, I teach them to make the right choices. I believe that freedom is a choice, that's why I named my mentoring organization after this belief. I believe it with everything in me. Regardless of what anybody else is doing, they know right from wrong, and I expect them to make the right decisions. Period. We've raised them right, and I'm confident they will do well in life. I love my sons, and I'm proud of these guys.

We are not thugs! We are men, we are educated, we are strong, we are Black and we are PROUD!

Omar and his sons: Deshan 24, Dequan 23 To contact Omar, Tweet him: @howard_omar

Andre Brown – Postal Delivery Driver

What are you teaching your son about racism?

My son is a high school junior with a 3.8 GPA at one of the best academically ranked schools in the city of Tuscaloosa, Alabama. He is also currently a Division I recruited athlete. It's tough being the parent of a Black male child in a society so openly hostile towards him; that sees him as an animal, and not as my baby boy, my pride and joy. Tuscaloosa has an extensive racially charged history, which dates back to the days of the legendary Paul "BEAR" Bryant deciding not to recruit African American Athletes due to the "social climate" of the University of Alabama. I made it my purpose to take my son to the Dr. Martin Luther King Jr. exhibit in Atlanta, before some field trip performed that parenting duty for me. I feel that I have instilled in him a divine dignity, the rewards of perseverance, as well as a humble conscience to analyze every trial he is faced with in life. I have compared and contrasted the differences between the wants of a boy in today's society as well as the needs of a young man in the spiritual sense. I have taught Jahi humility as well as sarcasm in the face of racism. I have also displayed the character in the face of adversity for him to emulate if provoked by ignorance.

Above: My son Jahi and I in Vegas waiting to ride the "Stratosphere". Below: Beaming with pride after the game! My son caught an interception to win the game. Go Hillcrest Patriots!

**Leonard Jones – AKA "Big Len"
Human Rights Activist & Talk Radio Show Host**

What do you teach your kids about racism?

I teach my kids that racism is an unfortunate part of our society based on the need of some White people to feel superior based on the color of skin. Ethnicity itself is not destructive, but the system of racism is prevalent in our culture and has caused a lot of pain and suffering in the Black community. Despite a legacy of issues associated with racism, Black people have made great strides in gaining full citizenship and access to all the opportunities necessary to live abundant lives. It is very important to me that my children understand that it is their responsibility to be productive citizens and involved in continuing the efforts of our ancestors to succeed regardless of the obstacles that may be placed in their way.

How have you overcome racism?

I have been able to overcome the majority of direct racism by educating myself on my civil and human rights. In addition to education, I also participate in my community as an activist and advocate for others. I do not believe that racism can be completely overcome, however I try to implement the best practices to confront racism and resolve those issues that help my family, and the community as a whole.

Leonard and his family: Chantel, Gralin and Jason.
Tweet Him: @hiphopspeaksliv

Jarius McDaniel – Community Leader, Activist, & Commercial Driver

Have you had a racist or discriminatory incident that shaped you or your thoughts on racism?

I grew up in an all Black area, then I left and went to a predominately White area in middle school (7th grade). Due to my inexperience with people from another ethnic group, and my naivety, I was subjected to discrimination, and didn't realize it at first. There were only two Black kids in my school, and White students always called me "Leroy". They weren't malicious, so I didn't know it was derogatory until I went home and told my dad. My dad told me that I should never let anyone call me anything other than my name, and explained to me why it was wrong. Another incident in the same school, taught me about the n-word.

I had a kid who took my lunchbox, slammed it on my desk, and called me a n-word. I was upset that the kid took my lunchbox, so I took his, and the teacher sent both of us to the principal's office. I had no idea that the n-word was bad, because it was used as a term of endearment in my old community. In the principal's office, the kid admitted with pride that he called me the n-word. The principal and staff were shocked and appalled, told me to go back to class, and I never saw that kid again. Apparently, someone explained to the other kids in my class about the word. They were welcoming when I returned, and I was never called the n-word or "Leroy" again in that school. Those incidents (and many others like them) made me bold, courageous, and unwilling to tolerate racist people or discrimination in any form. When I see it, I "nip it in the bud", and check it right there on the spot. I have seen other people be submissive to and fearful of White people, when I was working in the deep south. I hated the way it looked, and I will I will never walk in a spirit of fear or inferiority to any ethnic group. I believe in lifting up all people, and treating everyone with the utmost dignity and respect. That is what I expect from other people, and I do not accept anything less.

How have you overcome racism?

Overcome? There is no overcoming racism. You cannot overcome someone else's sick logic. You learn how to face it, when to avoid it, and how to deal with it. You learn how to enjoy your life and prosper in spite of it. I try to encourage other people to recognize racism for what it is, and to stand tall against it. I'm trying to overcome the self-hatred that Black people have within our own community, that has been deeply ingrained in many of us through White supremacy. We as Black people must understand what racism has done to us, refuse to accept the submissive position that some pastors and some community leaders often take. We have to network within our community to make it better.

Charles Muhammad – Community Leader & Activist

What do you teach your children about racism?
In dealing with racism with my sons, I have never put on the facade of "unicorns and cotton candy clouds." I have always tried to inform them of the deep harsh reality of institutionalized racism, which happens to unfortunately be the foundation of this country. I love to them the unadulterated truth of what it means to be a Black Man in America. I have tried to show them to "the subtle" and "the overt."

It is important to know that racism denotes "power and control," therefore to thwart this ugly stain, I've instilled in my sons to forge a way for themselves as opposed to "get in where they fit in" in a world is diametrically opposed to their very existence. Independent, creative thinking, outside the realm of "the establishment," is a must in raising our Black youth today.

To this end I've emphasized a knowledge of "self and kind." I've always told them to hold their heads up high and to be proud of themselves and their rich history. I've emphasized that to be Black and proud does not equate to being disrespectful to any other race. My motto to them has always been in order to truly appreciate others, you must love, embrace, and bask in the glory of who you are as a Blackman.

Fred Newell – Construction Worker & U.S. Marine Ret.

What do you teach your kids about racism?

I teach my kids that we don't judge by race. We are all God's children. That being said, my boys, now men, have had small run-ins with racism. My daughter is an emotional girl, who just loves people. But for this country's racial problem, it pisses me off that I have to teach her the truth of race problems. Because she is a Black girl, I know she will have a run-in with a racist person at least once in her life time.

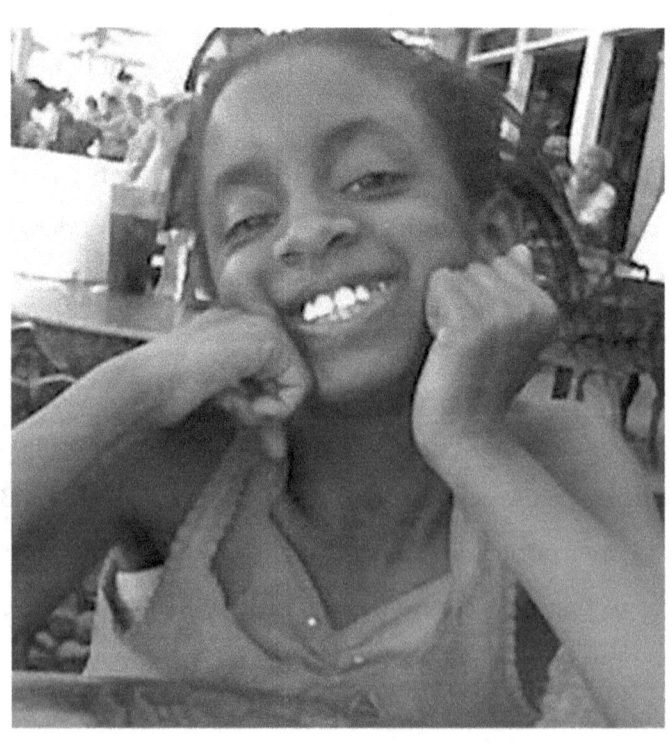

Tone X – Comedian & Actor

What do you teach your kids about race and racism?

I teach my sons the "*truth*" about racism. I always say information is the "*new currency*" - so I give them the information they don't get in their schools or from their teachers during Black History Month. I let my son's know "*where*" they come from and "*what*" they come from. I let them know it's not what "people" call you, it's what you answer to! I also work hard at being an example for them to follow, and being the one that shows them how to be a strong Black Man.

How did a racist incident shape you thoughts on racism?

I've spoken to my boys about how racism affected me when I did a show in Valdosta, Georgia years ago. One night on stage I got called a n***** by someone in the audience (a White man) and little did I know he happened to be a police officer. Of course my wisdom and understanding of who "I am" as a Black man gave me the advantage with my reply. Long story short, he became the joke of the night and highly regretted interrupting my show set. This incident stuck in my mind and it caused me to understand that racism existed way before me and will still exist after me - because racism is a mindset and it's a mentality, therefore people have to learn how to rise above the mentality and rise above the hate! The way you deal with it is by speaking truth to power and that's what I try to teach to my sons every day. As Fathers and Black Men we have to protect and educate our children. Every day I tell my sons you have to speak truth to power, ask questions, be smart and be aware.

To contact Tone X, Tweet him: @ToneXComedy

Troy Bishop - Psychotherapist

How has racism affected you?

I have been affected immensely by racism even before I was born, and permanently since I was born.

I was born in Tuscaloosa, Alabama on October 26, 1945. During that time it was commonly believed and practiced among the White citizens, that Blacks – Negroes as we were called at the time- were at best third class citizens but commonly thought of as inferior human beings. They thought we had inferior intelligence and that we were incapable of learning. We were thought of as beasts of labor, servants and that we ought to be slaves.

I was routinely referred to as "boy", not called even by my first name by Whites. Of course, for all of my teenage years, everything was segregated. The movies, the churches, the restaurants, water fountains, buses, etc. I even had to step off the side walk if a White person was approaching. I could not look a White man in the eyes or get physically close to a White woman. We were expected to address young White kids as "Mister" or "Miss".

Some of the more hurtful and traumatizing experiences includes several incidents where I was hired to work one or several days for a White woman cutting down bushes, trees, cleaning large cluttered storage houses, cutting grass, moving bricks and piles of dirt and rubbish. Only to be told when the work was finished and I asked for the payment they promised, "Nigger get the hell off my property! The only thing you will get is a bullet between your eyes, get yourself hung, or in jail".

Another traumatic experience was to observe my father, who was a very strong and proud man, be humiliated in front of me by a White man. We later found out that the man was a known klansman, who my father borrowed money from. Yet another traumatic experience which more than anything else motivated me to get a college education was the incredible ordeal and miscarriage of justice and violation of civil rights. When my 12th grade class went to vote, all the White kids had to do was state their name, age, address, sign on the line, and be gone. The Blacks were not given registration forms. We were made to wait several HOURS, had to recite the number of counties in the state, provide the district number for Tuscaloosa County, state the mayor, state the governor, and read the entire state constitution before we were permitted to register to vote.

During the 1960's, my mother was so afraid for my life that she physically restrained me from participating in as many marches, sit-ins, and protests as she could. However, those were the only times in my life that I willfully disobeyed my mom. She was one of God's most loving mothers.

After graduating from Stillman College with a B.A. in Sociology – Double minor in Psychology and World History, I could not get a job in Tuscaloosa as a social worker. However, I had two job offers in Cleveland, Ohio after a job recruiter came to our campus. In Cleveland, I easily became a social worker and case supervisor before I earned my Master's degree in social science administration. I worked for a few years as a supervisor, and returned to Tuscaloosa. I took a position as a social worker, because they would not hire me as a supervisor. Five years later the pattern of discrimination became even more clear. Two of the social workers in my unit, one with a Bachelors of social work (BSW) and one still in college working on a BSW were promoted to be my supervisor. I already had a bachelor's degree, a master's degree, and years of experience in the field as a social worker and as a supervisor, but because they were White, they were promoted over me. It would take five more years with outstanding skill and recognition from community, clientele, and colleagues that I was promoted to supervisor.

Why did you tolerate racism? How did you overcome racism?

I had two of God's most precious little daughters who deserved the best that I could give them. They were worth the indignities, insults, and heartbreak. Just like my mom. She broke my heart to keep me alive so I could give those two precious girls more than I had --- a better, more just world. Unfortunately we are not there yet. Thank God we are not where we used to be, but be assured, racism is alive and well. However, it is more subtle --- in education, finance, employment, politics, law enforcement, court systems, etc.

Above: Troy and youngest daughter, Troya. Below: Granddaughter, Zoe, 12 years old

THE ANSWERS: A Parent's Guide to Discussing Racism with Children

References

1. Allport, G. W. (1954). *The nature of prejudice.* Cambridge, MA: Addison-Wesley.

2. Andrews, G. (2016, January 1). *Grown ass man chronicles: Are you the problem or the solution?* Retrieved from http://www.gamchronicles.com/category/manhood/

3. Angelou, M., Neufeld, J.M. (January 16, 2011). *Oprah's Master Class.* Harpo Studios. Chicago, Il.

4. American Psychological Association. (2015 December 17). Retrieved from http://www.apa.org/about/gr/issues/health-care/disparities.aspx

5. Bigler, R.S., Wright, Y.F. (2014). Reading, writing, arithmetic, and racism? Risks and benefits to teaching children about intergroup biases. *Child Development Perspectives,* 8 (1) 18–23.

6. Brockner, J., De Cremer, D., Van den Bos, K., & Chen, Y.-R. (2005). The influence of interdependent self-construal on procedural fairness effects. *Organizational Behavior and Human Decision Processes,* 96, 155–167.

7. Brookfield, S.D. (2004). Critical thinking techniques. In M.W. Galbraith. *Adult learning methods: A guide for effective instruction.* (341-360). Malabar, Fl.

8. Bryant-Davis, T., & Ocampo, C. (2005). Racist incident based trauma. *Counseling Psychologist, 33,* 479-500

9. Buckley, T. R., & Carter, R. T. (2005). Black adolescent girls: Do gender role and racial identity impact their self-esteem? *Sex Roles.* (53) 647–666.

10. Carter, R. T. (2007). Racism and psychological and emotional injury: Recognizing and assessing race-based traumatic stress. *The Counseling Psychologist*, 35 (1) 13-105.

11. De Cremer, D., & Tyler, T. R. (2005). Managing group behavior: The interplay between procedural fairness, self, and cooperation. In M. Zanna (Ed.), *Advances in experimental social psychology*. (37) 152–218. New York, NY: Academic Press.

12. Degner, J., Dalege, J. (2013). The apple does not fall far from the tree, or does it? A meta-analysis of parent–child similarity in intergroup attitudes. *American Psychological Association*. 139, (6) 1270–1304.

13. Dekalb, C. (2015, August 27). *Welcome to Dekalb*. Retrieved from http://web.dekalbcountyga.gov/decidedekalb/ed-school-system.html

14. Garland, S. (2015, December 9). Bloom's taxonomy: Critical thinking for kids. Retrieved from http://www.exquisite-minds.com/idea-of-the-week/blooms-taxonomy-critical-thinking-skills/

15. Glaser, J.E. (2014). *Conversational Intelligence: How great leaders build trust and get extraordinary results*. Brookline, MA. Bibliomotion, Inc.

16. Goldsmith, M. (2015). *Triggers: How to create behavior change that lasts*. New York, NY. Crown Publishing Group.

17. Gushue, G.V., Mejia-Smith, B. X., Fisher, L. D., Cogger, A., Gonzalez-Matthews, M., Lee, Y.J., Mancusi, L., McCullough, R., Connell, M. T., Weng, W.C., Cheng, M., Johnson, V. (2013). Differentiation of self and racial identity. *Counseling Psychology Quarterly*. 26 (3–4) 343–361.

18. Haslam, N. (2006). Dehumanization: An integrative review. *Personality and Social Psychology Review*. (10) 252–264.

19. Helms, J. E. (1995). An update of Helms' white and people of color racial identity models. In J. G. Ponterotto, J. M. Casas, L. A. Suzuki, & C. M. Alexander (Eds.), Handbook of multicultural counseling 181–198. Thousand Oaks, CA: Sage.

20. Helms, J.E., Nicholas, G., Green, C.E. (2012). Racism and ethnoviolence as trauma: Enhancing professional and research training. *Traumatology.* 18 (1) 65-74.

21. Hoyt, C. (2005). Wiping out prejudices before they start. *Parents Magazine.* Retrieved from http://www.parents.com/parenting/better-parenting/teaching-tolerance/wiping-out-kid-prejudices-before-they-start/

22. Johnson, R.E., Lord, R.G. (2010). Implicit effects of justice on self-identity. *Journal of Applied Psychology.* 95 (4) 681– 695.

23. Kennedy-Moore, E. (2015). How not to raise a narcissist: What really causes narcissism in children and how parents can help. *Psychology Today.* Retreived from https://www.psychologytoday.com/blog/growing-friendships/201503/how-not-raise-narcissist

24. Lane, J. (2008). Young children and racial justice: Taking action for racial equality in the early years – understanding the past, thinking about the present, planning for the future. *National Children's Bureau.*

25. Lemley, K. (2014). Social justice in teacher education: Naming discrimination to promote transformative action. *Critical Questions in Education.* 5 (1) 26-51.

26. Lind, E. A. (2001). Fairness heuristic theory: Justice judgments as pivotal cognitions in organizational relations. In J. Greenberg & R. Cropanzano (Eds.), *Advances in*

organizational justice. (56 – 88). San Francisco, CA: New Lexington Press.

27. Livingstone- Smith, D. (2011). Less than human: *Why we demean, enslave, and exterminate others.* New York, NY: St. Martin's Press.

28. Markus, H.R., (2008). Pride, prejudice, and ambivalence: Toward a unified theory of race and ethnicity. *American Psychologist.* 651-670.

29. Merriam-Webster. (2015, November 3). *Oppression.* Retrieved from http://www.merriam-webster.com/dictionary/oppression

30. Merriam-Webster. (2015, November 3). *Poverty.* Retrieved from http://www.merriam-webster.com/dictionary/poverty

31. Miller, J.D., Maples, J. L., Buffardi, L., Huajian, C., Gentile, B., Kisbu-Sakarya, Y., Kwan, V.S.Y., LoPilato, A., Pendry, L.F., Sedikides, C., Seidor, L., Campbell, W.K. (2015). Narcissism and United States' culture: The view from home and around the world. *Journal of Personality and Social Psychology.* 109. (6) 1068 –1089.

32. National Human Genome Research Institute. (2015, August 30). *Frequently asked questions about genetic and genomic science.* Retrieved from http://www.genome.gov/19016904

33. Nghe, L. T., & Mahalik, J. R. (2001). Examining racial identity status as predictors of psychological defenses in African American college students. *Journal of Counseling Psychology.* (48) 10–16.

34. Parham, A. A. (2008). Race memory and family history. *Social Identities.* 14 (1) 13-32.

35. Pinola, M. (2015 November 17). How to talk to about race to

your kids. Retrieved from http://lifehacker.com/how-to-talk-about-race-with-your-kids-1681298311

36. Plante, T.G. (2013). How to spot a narcissist: Pretty easy when everywhere. *Psychology Today*. Retrieved from https://www.psychologytoday.com/blog/do-the-right-thing/201308/how-spot-narcissist-pretty-easy-when-everywhere

37. Price-Mitchell, M. (2015 December 9). Critical thinking: How to grow your child's mind. Retrieved from http://www.rootsofaction.com/critical-thinking-ways-to-improve-your-childs-mind-this-summer/

38. *Psychology Today*. (2015 December 19). Retrieved from https://www.psychologytoday.com/conditions/narcissistic-personality-disorder

39. Raabe, T., Beelmann, A. (2011). Development of ethnic, racial, and national prejudice in childhood and adolescence: A multinational meta-analysis of age differences. *Child Development*. 82 (6) 1715-1737.

40. Smedley, A. (2015, August 31). *American anthropological association position paper on race*. Retrieved from http://www.aaanet.org/stmts/racepp.htm

41. Smiley, R. (2015, August 30). Angie Stone explains how 'Brotha' is relevant now more than ever. *Rickey Smiley Morning Show*. Retrieved from http://rickeysmileymorningshow.com/1564227/new-angie-stone-brotha-video/

42. Speicher, L. (2014). Microaggressions. [Powerpoint slides]. Retrieved from http://www.slideboom.com/presentations/513612/Wk3-Microagressions---Lecture-2_Speicher

43. Sue, D.W., Capodilupo, C.M., Torino, G.C., Bucceri, J.M., Holder, A.M.B., Nadal, K.L., Esquilin, M. (2007). Racial microaggressions in everyday life: Implications for clinical practice. *American Psychologist*, 62(4), 271-286.

44. Tatum, B. D. (1999). *Why are all the Black kids sitting together in the cafeteria?: And other conversations about race.* New York, NY: Basic Books.

45. Tyler, T. R., & Blader, S. L. (2003). The group engagement model: Procedural justice, social identity, and cooperative behavior. *Personality and Social Psychology Review*. (7). 349 –361.

46. Wise, T. (2015, August 27). *Frequently Asked Questions*. Retrieved from http://www.timwise.org/f-a-q-s/

47. Whittemore, K. (2015, November 20). Raising a child who respects difference. *Parents Magazine*. Retrieved from http://www.parents.com/parenting/better-parenting/teaching-tolerance/raising-a-child-who-respects-difference/

48. Williams, M.T. (2013). Can racism cause PTSD: Implications for DSM-5. *Psychology Today*. Retrieved from https://www.psychologytoday.com/blog/culturally-speaking/201305/can-racism-cause-ptsd-implications-dsm-5

49. Williams, M.T. (2015). The link between racism and PTSD: A psychologist explains race-based stress and trauma in Black Americans. *Psychology Today*. Retrieved from

https://www.psychologytoday.com/blog/culturally-speaking/201509/the-link-between-racism-and-ptsd

50. Zerubavel, E. (1996). Social memories: Steps to a sociology of the past. *Qualitative Sociology.* 19 (3) 283-299.

51. Zigler, Z. (2015 December 18). The answer to racism. *Creators.com.* Retrieved from http://www.creators.com/lifestylefeatures/inspiration/classic-zig-ziglar/the-answer-to-racism.html

THE ANSWERS: A Parent's Guide to Discussing Racism with Children

Troya Bishop, M. Ed.

ABOUT THE AUTHOR

Troya is regarded as a fierce fighter and advocate for social causes. With over 21 years of experience in advocacy and non-violent protests. She has extensive experience in long-term strategic planning, with various civil and human rights organizations.

Troya has been active in the social justice movement since attending NAACP meetings in Tuscaloosa, Alabama as a child. Tapped as a natural leader, she served in various leadership roles, as she continued to acquire more skills to become the best person, and leader possible. She served as a Leadership Commissioner (2010-2012) and Crisis Committee Chairperson in Rev. Al Sharpton's Atlanta office of National Action Network (2009-2012). Under the leadership of Rev. Sharpton, Troya was a key liaison in many cases regarding human rights violations. She was key in the mobilization effort to stop Troy Davis' execution by coordinating press campaigns, rallies, protests, and collaborating with many other organizations. She often speaks of the horror she felt and trauma she experienced after being at the prison with Troy's family and other activists when he was executed.

As a believer in the nonviolent approach to crisis resolution, she identifies closely with the philosophies of Dr. King and Mahatma

Ghandi. Non-violent activism was a key approach to social change that she learned while earning her B.S. in Communications from Howard University. While completing her M. Ed. at Tennessee State University, her research was heavily comprised of (non-violent) strategies for working with children with behavior disorders. She is developing her skills to motivate and teach adults, as she earns her doctorate of education in Higher Education & Adult Learning from Walden University.

Other organizations that Troya is a member of, are: The Southern Poverty Law Center, Amnesty International, Council for Exceptional Children, A.R.O.M.A, Georgians for the Alternative to the Death Penalty, and many other justice coalitions. Motivated by her commitment to teaching adults to advocate for themselves, Troya started her own non-profit organization, Parental Empowerment Institute (PEI), in October of 2012. Troya's passion for obtaining justice and equality for all and her ability to work with people, earned her a permanent place in the movement, and a soft spot in the hearts of those she has served.

Contact the Author:

Twitter: @OleBadd

Facebook: Ole' Badd Troya

Instagram: @OleBadd

Email: TheAnswers2@hotmail.com

Troya Bishop, M. Ed.

DON'T FORGET TO USE YOUR WORKBOOK!

Purchase other Materials for your children & share your thoughts:
http://theanswers2.wix.com/answers
Twitter: @Answers2Racism
Facebook: Facebook.com/TheAnswersAParentsGuide
Email: TheAnswers2@hotmail.com

COMING SOON!

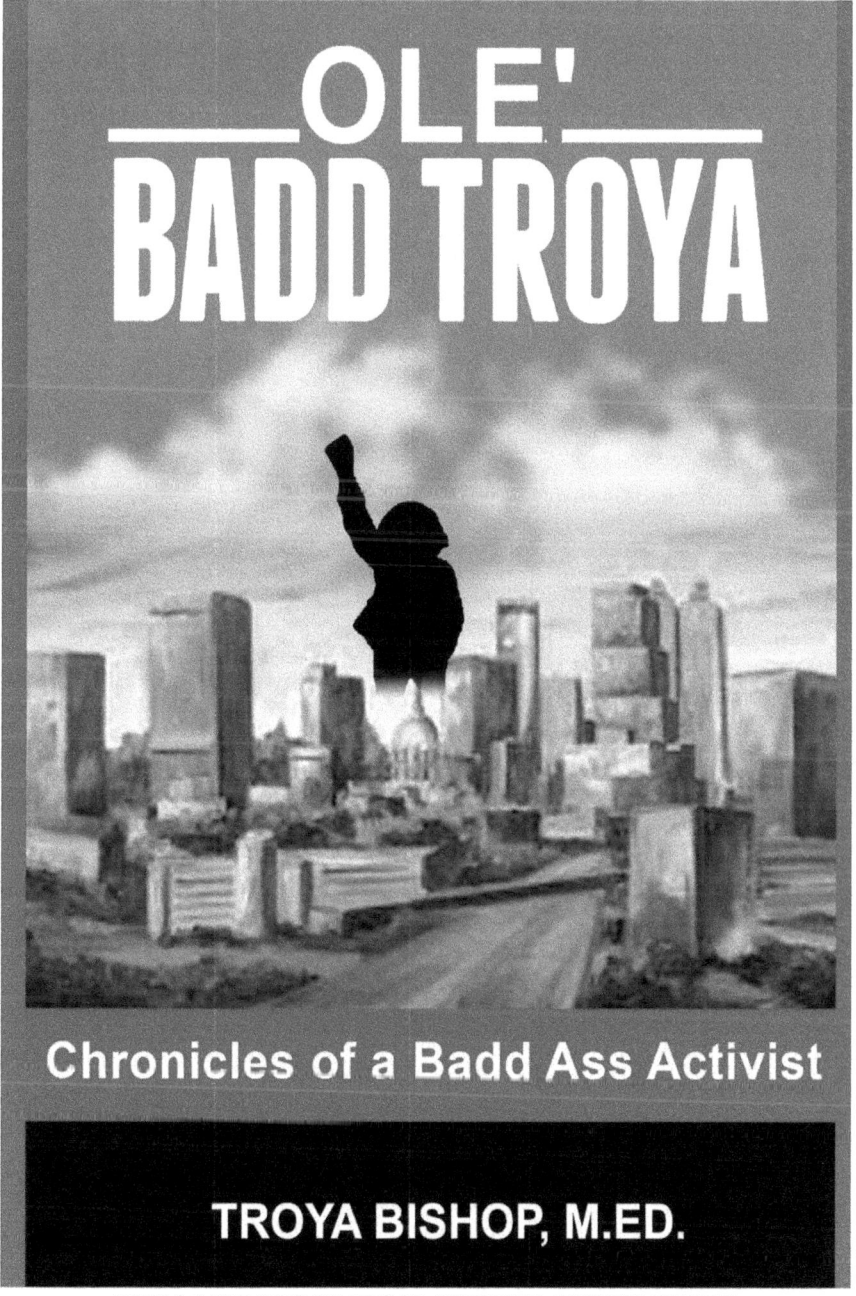

THANK YOU FOR YOUR SUPPORT!

www.ingramcontent.com/pod-product-compliance
Lightning Source LLC
Chambersburg PA
CBHW070248100426
42743CB00011B/2184